50 Delicious Dairy-Free Desserts Recipes

By: Kelly Johnson

Table of Contents

- Dairy-Free Chocolate Cake
- Vegan Chocolate Chip Cookies
- Coconut Macaroons
- Almond Milk Panna Cotta
- Apple Cinnamon Crumble
- Vegan Lemon Bars
- Dairy-Free Chocolate Mousse
- Dairy-Free Cheesecake
- Chia Pudding with Mixed Berries
- Vegan Rice Pudding
- Banana Ice Cream
- Dairy-Free Key Lime Pie
- Oatmeal Raisin Cookies
- Vegan Chocolate Brownies
- Coconut Milk Rice Pudding
- Raw Vegan Chocolate Fudge
- Strawberry Sorbet
- Dairy-Free Cinnamon Rolls
- Avocado Chocolate Pudding
- Coconut-Lime Cupcakes
- Vegan Pumpkin Pie
- Chocolate-Covered Frozen Bananas
- Dairy-Free Coconut Flan
- Vegan Carrot Cake
- Banana Bread (Dairy-Free)
- Vegan Coconut Cream Pie
- Chocolate-Dipped Strawberries
- Dairy-Free Scones
- Mango Coconut Sorbet
- Vegan Chocolate Truffles
- Pineapple Coconut Popsicles
- Dairy-Free Chocolate Tarts
- Peach Crisp with Oat Topping
- Almond Joy Energy Balls
- Vegan Lemon Coconut Bars

- Cashew Cream Pie
- Chocolate Coconut Energy Balls
- Apple Sorbet
- Vegan Chocolate Cupcakes
- Dairy-Free Coffee Ice Cream
- Chocolate Avocado Mousse
- Vegan Peanut Butter Cups
- Coconut Raspberry Tart
- Dairy-Free Blueberry Muffins
- Watermelon Sorbet
- Vegan Chocolate Chip Blondies
- Lemon Poppy Seed Cake
- Apple Cinnamon Donuts
- Vegan Mocha Pudding Cake
- Dairy-Free Chocolate Covered Almonds

Dairy-Free Chocolate Cake

Ingredients:

- 1 1/2 cups flour
- 1 cup sugar
- 1/2 cup cocoa powder
- 1 tsp baking soda
- 1/2 tsp baking powder
- 1/2 tsp salt
- 1 cup almond milk
- 1/2 cup vegetable oil
- 1 tsp vanilla extract
- 1 tbsp apple cider vinegar

Instructions:

1. Preheat oven to 350°F (175°C) and grease and flour an 8-inch cake pan.
2. In a large bowl, whisk together flour, sugar, cocoa powder, baking soda, baking powder, and salt.
3. Add almond milk, oil, vanilla extract, and apple cider vinegar. Stir until smooth.
4. Pour the batter into the prepared pan and bake for 30–35 minutes or until a toothpick inserted comes out clean.
5. Let the cake cool before frosting or serving.

Vegan Chocolate Chip Cookies

Ingredients:

- 1 1/2 cups flour
- 1/2 tsp baking soda
- 1/4 tsp salt
- 1/2 cup coconut oil, melted
- 1/4 cup maple syrup
- 1/4 cup almond milk
- 1 tsp vanilla extract
- 1 cup dairy-free chocolate chips

Instructions:

1. Preheat the oven to 350°F (175°C) and line a baking sheet with parchment paper.
2. In a medium bowl, whisk together flour, baking soda, and salt.
3. In another bowl, combine coconut oil, maple syrup, almond milk, and vanilla.
4. Add wet ingredients to dry ingredients and mix until combined. Fold in the chocolate chips.
5. Scoop spoonfuls of dough onto the baking sheet and bake for 8–10 minutes, or until golden brown.
6. Let cool on a wire rack before serving.

Coconut Macaroons

Ingredients:

- 2 1/2 cups shredded coconut
- 1/4 cup sugar
- 1/4 tsp salt
- 2 tbsp aquafaba (chickpea brine)
- 1 tsp vanilla extract
- 1/4 cup dairy-free chocolate chips (optional)

Instructions:

1. Preheat oven to 350°F (175°C) and line a baking sheet with parchment paper.
2. In a large bowl, mix shredded coconut, sugar, and salt.
3. Add aquafaba and vanilla extract, stirring until the mixture sticks together.
4. Form the mixture into small mounds and place them on the baking sheet.
5. Bake for 15–20 minutes until golden brown.
6. If desired, melt dairy-free chocolate chips and drizzle over cooled macaroons.

Almond Milk Panna Cotta

Ingredients:

- 2 cups almond milk
- 1/4 cup sugar
- 1 tbsp agar agar powder
- 1 tsp vanilla extract

Instructions:

1. In a saucepan, combine almond milk, sugar, and agar agar.
2. Bring to a simmer over medium heat, stirring constantly.
3. Once the mixture thickens, remove from heat and stir in vanilla extract.
4. Pour the mixture into ramekins or molds and refrigerate for 4 hours, or until set.
5. Serve with fresh berries or a fruit compote.

Apple Cinnamon Crumble

Ingredients:

- 4 apples, peeled and sliced
- 1 tbsp lemon juice
- 1 tsp cinnamon
- 1/2 cup oats
- 1/4 cup almond flour
- 2 tbsp coconut oil, melted
- 2 tbsp maple syrup

Instructions:

1. Preheat oven to 350°F (175°C) and grease a baking dish.
2. Toss apple slices with lemon juice and cinnamon, then place in the baking dish.
3. In a bowl, combine oats, almond flour, coconut oil, and maple syrup to form the crumble topping.
4. Sprinkle the topping evenly over the apples.
5. Bake for 30–35 minutes, or until the apples are tender and the topping is golden brown.

Vegan Lemon Bars

Ingredients:

- 1 1/2 cups flour
- 1/4 cup powdered sugar
- 1/2 cup coconut oil, softened
- 1 cup lemon juice
- 1/4 cup sugar
- 2 tbsp cornstarch
- 1/4 tsp turmeric (for color)

Instructions:

1. Preheat the oven to 350°F (175°C) and grease a baking pan.
2. For the crust, combine flour, powdered sugar, and coconut oil. Press the mixture into the bottom of the pan.
3. Bake for 10–12 minutes until lightly golden.
4. For the filling, whisk together lemon juice, sugar, cornstarch, and turmeric in a bowl.
5. Pour the mixture over the crust and bake for another 20–25 minutes until set.
6. Let cool before slicing into bars.

Dairy-Free Chocolate Mousse

Ingredients:

- 1 can coconut milk (full-fat)
- 1/4 cup dairy-free chocolate chips
- 1 tbsp maple syrup
- 1 tsp vanilla extract

Instructions:

1. Chill the coconut milk in the fridge for several hours or overnight.
2. Scoop the solidified coconut cream from the can and melt it with chocolate chips in a double boiler.
3. Whisk in maple syrup and vanilla extract.
4. Let the mixture cool slightly, then refrigerate for 2 hours.
5. Serve with whipped coconut cream or fresh berries.

Dairy-Free Cheesecake

Ingredients:

- 1 1/2 cups raw cashews, soaked
- 1/2 cup coconut oil, melted
- 1/4 cup maple syrup
- 1/4 cup lemon juice
- 1 tsp vanilla extract
- 1/2 cup almond flour (for crust)
- 2 tbsp coconut sugar (for crust)

Instructions:

1. Preheat oven to 350°F (175°C) and grease a springform pan.
2. For the crust, combine almond flour and coconut sugar, then press into the bottom of the pan. Bake for 8 minutes.
3. In a blender, combine soaked cashews, coconut oil, maple syrup, lemon juice, and vanilla. Blend until smooth.
4. Pour the filling onto the baked crust and refrigerate for 4 hours.
5. Serve topped with fresh fruit or fruit compote.

Chia Pudding with Mixed Berries

Ingredients:

- 1/2 cup chia seeds
- 2 cups almond milk (or any dairy-free milk)
- 1 tbsp maple syrup
- 1 tsp vanilla extract
- 1/2 cup mixed berries (blueberries, raspberries, strawberries)

Instructions:

1. In a bowl, whisk together chia seeds, almond milk, maple syrup, and vanilla extract.
2. Let the mixture sit for 5 minutes, then whisk again to prevent clumping.
3. Cover the bowl and refrigerate for at least 4 hours or overnight until thickened.
4. Before serving, top with mixed berries and enjoy!

Vegan Rice Pudding

Ingredients:

- 1 cup cooked rice
- 2 1/2 cups almond milk (or any dairy-free milk)
- 1/4 cup maple syrup
- 1 tsp vanilla extract
- 1/2 tsp cinnamon
- 1/4 tsp nutmeg

Instructions:

1. In a saucepan, combine cooked rice and almond milk.
2. Bring to a simmer over medium heat, stirring occasionally.
3. Add maple syrup, vanilla extract, cinnamon, and nutmeg. Stir until well combined.
4. Cook for 15–20 minutes, stirring often, until the mixture thickens to a creamy consistency.
5. Serve warm or chilled.

Banana Ice Cream

Ingredients:

- 3 ripe bananas, peeled and sliced
- 1 tsp vanilla extract
- 1 tbsp almond milk (optional)

Instructions:

1. Place sliced bananas in a freezer-safe container and freeze for at least 2 hours or overnight.
2. Blend frozen banana slices in a food processor or blender until smooth and creamy.
3. Add vanilla extract and almond milk if the mixture is too thick.
4. Serve immediately for soft-serve consistency or freeze for 1–2 hours for a firmer texture.

Dairy-Free Key Lime Pie

Ingredients:

- 1 1/2 cups raw cashews, soaked for 4 hours
- 1/2 cup coconut cream
- 1/4 cup lime juice
- 2 tbsp maple syrup
- 1 tsp vanilla extract
- 1 1/2 cups graham cracker crumbs (gluten-free if needed)
- 1/4 cup coconut oil, melted

Instructions:

1. Preheat oven to 350°F (175°C).
2. For the crust, combine graham cracker crumbs and melted coconut oil, then press into the bottom of a pie pan. Bake for 10 minutes and set aside to cool.
3. For the filling, blend soaked cashews, coconut cream, lime juice, maple syrup, and vanilla extract until smooth and creamy.
4. Pour the filling onto the cooled crust and refrigerate for at least 4 hours, or overnight.
5. Serve chilled, garnished with lime zest.

Oatmeal Raisin Cookies

Ingredients:

- 1 cup rolled oats
- 1/2 cup almond flour
- 1/4 cup coconut sugar
- 1/2 tsp baking soda
- 1/2 tsp cinnamon
- 1/4 tsp salt
- 1/4 cup coconut oil, melted
- 1/4 cup maple syrup
- 1 tsp vanilla extract
- 1/2 cup raisins

Instructions:

1. Preheat the oven to 350°F (175°C) and line a baking sheet with parchment paper.
2. In a large bowl, combine oats, almond flour, coconut sugar, baking soda, cinnamon, and salt.
3. Stir in melted coconut oil, maple syrup, and vanilla extract.
4. Fold in raisins.
5. Scoop tablespoon-sized portions of dough onto the baking sheet and bake for 8–10 minutes, or until golden brown.
6. Let the cookies cool on a wire rack before serving.

Vegan Chocolate Brownies

Ingredients:

- 1 cup almond flour
- 1/4 cup cocoa powder
- 1/2 tsp baking soda
- 1/4 tsp salt
- 1/4 cup coconut oil, melted
- 1/4 cup maple syrup
- 1 tsp vanilla extract
- 1/4 cup dairy-free chocolate chips

Instructions:

1. Preheat oven to 350°F (175°C) and line a baking pan with parchment paper.
2. In a bowl, combine almond flour, cocoa powder, baking soda, and salt.
3. Add melted coconut oil, maple syrup, and vanilla extract, and stir until well combined.
4. Fold in chocolate chips.
5. Pour the batter into the prepared pan and bake for 20–25 minutes.
6. Let cool before cutting into squares and serving.

Coconut Milk Rice Pudding

Ingredients:

- 1 cup cooked rice
- 1 can (13.5 oz) coconut milk
- 1/4 cup maple syrup
- 1 tsp vanilla extract
- 1/2 tsp cinnamon
- 1/4 tsp nutmeg

Instructions:

1. In a saucepan, combine cooked rice and coconut milk.
2. Bring to a simmer over medium heat, stirring occasionally.
3. Add maple syrup, vanilla extract, cinnamon, and nutmeg.
4. Cook for 15–20 minutes, stirring often, until the mixture thickens to a creamy consistency.
5. Serve warm or chilled.

Raw Vegan Chocolate Fudge

Ingredients:

- 1 cup raw almonds
- 1/2 cup raw cacao powder
- 1/4 cup maple syrup
- 1/4 cup coconut oil, melted
- 1/2 tsp vanilla extract

Instructions:

1. In a food processor, blend almonds until they form a crumbly texture.
2. Add cacao powder, maple syrup, coconut oil, and vanilla extract, then process until the mixture is well combined and sticky.
3. Press the mixture into a lined baking dish and refrigerate for at least 2 hours.
4. Once set, cut into small squares and serve chilled.

Strawberry Sorbet

Ingredients:

- 4 cups fresh strawberries, hulled
- 1/2 cup coconut water or fruit juice
- 1/4 cup maple syrup (or sweetener of choice)
- 1 tbsp lemon juice

Instructions:

1. Blend the strawberries, coconut water, maple syrup, and lemon juice in a food processor or blender until smooth.
2. Pour the mixture into a shallow pan and freeze for about 4 hours, stirring every 30 minutes to break up any ice crystals.
3. Once the sorbet is firm and smooth, scoop and serve immediately.

Dairy-Free Cinnamon Rolls

Ingredients:

- 1 1/2 cups almond milk (or any dairy-free milk)
- 1/4 cup coconut oil, melted
- 2 tbsp sugar
- 2 1/4 tsp active dry yeast
- 4 cups all-purpose flour
- 1/2 tsp salt
- 1 tsp cinnamon
- 1/4 cup maple syrup
- 1/4 cup coconut sugar

Instructions:

1. Warm the almond milk and stir in coconut oil and sugar. Sprinkle the yeast over the milk and let it sit for 5–10 minutes.
2. In a large bowl, mix flour and salt. Add the yeast mixture and stir until a dough forms.
3. Knead the dough for about 5 minutes, then let it rise for 1 hour or until doubled in size.
4. Roll the dough into a rectangle, spread maple syrup and coconut sugar, and sprinkle cinnamon.
5. Roll the dough up tightly, slice into individual rolls, and place on a baking tray.
6. Bake at 350°F (175°C) for 20–25 minutes, until golden brown.

Avocado Chocolate Pudding

Ingredients:

- 2 ripe avocados, peeled and pitted
- 1/4 cup cocoa powder
- 1/4 cup maple syrup
- 1 tsp vanilla extract
- 1/4 cup almond milk (or any dairy-free milk)
- Pinch of salt

Instructions:

1. Blend the avocados, cocoa powder, maple syrup, vanilla extract, almond milk, and salt in a food processor or blender until smooth.
2. Adjust sweetness to taste and refrigerate for 1–2 hours.
3. Serve chilled, topped with berries or coconut flakes if desired.

Coconut-Lime Cupcakes

Ingredients:

- 1 1/2 cups all-purpose flour
- 1/2 cup coconut sugar
- 1 tsp baking powder
- 1/2 tsp baking soda
- 1/4 tsp salt
- 1/2 cup coconut milk
- 1/4 cup coconut oil, melted
- 1 tbsp lime juice
- 1 tsp lime zest
- 1 tsp vanilla extract

Instructions:

1. Preheat oven to 350°F (175°C) and line a muffin tin with paper liners.
2. In a bowl, combine flour, coconut sugar, baking powder, baking soda, and salt.
3. In another bowl, mix coconut milk, coconut oil, lime juice, lime zest, and vanilla extract.
4. Stir wet ingredients into dry ingredients until just combined.
5. Pour the batter into the muffin tin and bake for 18–20 minutes, until a toothpick inserted comes out clean.

Vegan Pumpkin Pie

Ingredients:

- 1 can (15 oz) pumpkin puree
- 1/2 cup coconut milk
- 1/4 cup maple syrup
- 2 tbsp cornstarch
- 1 tsp cinnamon
- 1/2 tsp ginger
- 1/4 tsp nutmeg
- 1/4 tsp salt
- 1 tsp vanilla extract
- 1 pre-made vegan pie crust

Instructions:

1. Preheat oven to 350°F (175°C).
2. In a blender, combine pumpkin puree, coconut milk, maple syrup, cornstarch, spices, salt, and vanilla extract. Blend until smooth.
3. Pour the filling into the vegan pie crust and smooth the top.
4. Bake for 40–45 minutes, until the filling is set and a toothpick inserted comes out clean.
5. Let cool for at least 2 hours before serving.

Chocolate-Covered Frozen Bananas

Ingredients:

- 3 ripe bananas, peeled and cut into 1-inch slices
- 1 cup dairy-free chocolate chips
- 1 tbsp coconut oil

Instructions:

1. Place banana slices on a parchment-lined baking sheet and freeze for 1–2 hours.
2. Melt the chocolate chips and coconut oil in a double boiler or microwave.
3. Dip each frozen banana slice into the melted chocolate, then return to the baking sheet.
4. Freeze again for 1 hour until the chocolate is firm. Serve immediately or store in the freezer.

Dairy-Free Coconut Flan

Ingredients:

- 1 can (14 oz) coconut milk
- 1/2 cup coconut sugar
- 2 tbsp cornstarch
- 1 tsp vanilla extract
- 1/4 tsp salt
- 1/2 tsp agar-agar powder (for setting)

Instructions:

1. In a saucepan, combine coconut milk, coconut sugar, and cornstarch. Cook over medium heat, whisking constantly until it thickens.
2. Add vanilla extract, salt, and agar-agar powder, stirring until well combined.
3. Pour the mixture into small ramekins and refrigerate for at least 4 hours to set.
4. Serve chilled, topped with fresh fruit or caramel sauce.

Vegan Carrot Cake

Ingredients:

- 1 1/2 cups whole wheat flour
- 1/2 cup coconut sugar
- 1 tsp baking soda
- 1/2 tsp baking powder
- 1 tsp cinnamon
- 1/2 tsp nutmeg
- 1/4 tsp salt
- 2 cups grated carrots
- 1/2 cup coconut oil, melted
- 1/2 cup almond milk
- 1 tsp vanilla extract

Instructions:

1. Preheat oven to 350°F (175°C) and line a cake pan with parchment paper.
2. In a bowl, mix flour, coconut sugar, baking soda, baking powder, cinnamon, nutmeg, and salt.
3. Stir in grated carrots, melted coconut oil, almond milk, and vanilla extract.
4. Pour the batter into the prepared cake pan and bake for 25–30 minutes, or until a toothpick inserted comes out clean.
5. Let the cake cool completely before frosting with vegan cream cheese or coconut whipped cream.

Banana Bread (Dairy-Free)

Ingredients:

- 3 ripe bananas, mashed
- 1/2 cup coconut oil, melted
- 1/2 cup maple syrup or honey
- 2 cups all-purpose flour
- 1 tsp baking soda
- 1/2 tsp salt
- 1 tsp cinnamon
- 1 tsp vanilla extract
- 1/2 cup almond milk (or any dairy-free milk)

Instructions:

1. Preheat oven to 350°F (175°C) and grease a loaf pan.
2. In a large bowl, mash the bananas and mix in the coconut oil, maple syrup, and vanilla extract.
3. In another bowl, combine the flour, baking soda, salt, and cinnamon.
4. Add the dry ingredients to the wet ingredients, alternating with almond milk, and stir until just combined.
5. Pour the batter into the loaf pan and bake for 50-60 minutes, or until a toothpick comes out clean.
6. Let cool before slicing and serving.

Vegan Coconut Cream Pie

Ingredients:

- 1 pre-made vegan pie crust
- 1 can (13.5 oz) coconut milk
- 1/4 cup cornstarch
- 1/4 cup maple syrup
- 1 tsp vanilla extract
- 1/2 cup shredded coconut
- Vegan whipped cream for topping

Instructions:

1. Preheat oven to 350°F (175°C) and bake the pie crust according to package instructions.
2. In a saucepan, whisk together coconut milk, cornstarch, and maple syrup over medium heat.
3. Cook, stirring constantly, until the mixture thickens. Once thickened, remove from heat and stir in vanilla extract and shredded coconut.
4. Pour the coconut mixture into the pie crust and refrigerate for at least 4 hours, or until set.
5. Top with vegan whipped cream and extra shredded coconut before serving.

Chocolate-Dipped Strawberries

Ingredients:

- 1 pint fresh strawberries, hulled
- 1 cup dairy-free chocolate chips
- 1 tbsp coconut oil

Instructions:

1. Melt the chocolate chips and coconut oil in a microwave-safe bowl in 30-second intervals, stirring in between.
2. Dip each strawberry into the melted chocolate, covering about 3/4 of the strawberry.
3. Place the dipped strawberries on a parchment-lined tray and refrigerate until the chocolate hardens (about 30 minutes).
4. Serve immediately or store in the fridge.

Dairy-Free Scones

Ingredients:

- 2 cups all-purpose flour
- 1/4 cup coconut sugar
- 1 tbsp baking powder
- 1/2 tsp salt
- 1/2 cup coconut oil, cold
- 1/2 cup almond milk
- 1 tsp vanilla extract
- 1/2 cup dried fruit or dairy-free chocolate chips (optional)

Instructions:

1. Preheat oven to 375°F (190°C) and line a baking sheet with parchment paper.
2. In a large bowl, whisk together flour, coconut sugar, baking powder, and salt.
3. Cut in the cold coconut oil until the mixture resembles coarse crumbs.
4. Stir in the almond milk and vanilla extract, then fold in dried fruit or chocolate chips, if desired.
5. Turn the dough onto a floured surface, gently knead, and shape into a disc. Cut into 8 wedges and place on the baking sheet.
6. Bake for 15-20 minutes, or until golden brown.

Mango Coconut Sorbet

Ingredients:

- 3 ripe mangos, peeled and diced
- 1/2 cup coconut milk
- 1/4 cup lime juice
- 2 tbsp maple syrup or agave syrup

Instructions:

1. Blend the mango, coconut milk, lime juice, and maple syrup in a blender until smooth.
2. Pour the mixture into a shallow container and freeze for 3-4 hours, stirring every 30 minutes to prevent ice crystals from forming.
3. Once the sorbet is frozen and smooth, serve immediately or store in the freezer.

Vegan Chocolate Truffles

Ingredients:

- 1 cup dairy-free chocolate chips
- 1/4 cup coconut cream
- 1/2 tsp vanilla extract
- Cocoa powder or shredded coconut for rolling

Instructions:

1. Heat the coconut cream in a saucepan over medium heat until it begins to simmer.
2. Pour the hot coconut cream over the chocolate chips in a heatproof bowl. Stir until the chocolate is melted and smooth.
3. Stir in vanilla extract and refrigerate the mixture for 1-2 hours, until firm enough to scoop.
4. Scoop out spoonfuls of the chocolate mixture and roll into balls. Roll the truffles in cocoa powder or shredded coconut.
5. Refrigerate until set and serve.

Pineapple Coconut Popsicles

Ingredients:

- 2 cups fresh pineapple, diced
- 1/2 cup coconut milk
- 2 tbsp maple syrup or agave syrup
- 1/4 cup shredded coconut

Instructions:

1. Blend the pineapple, coconut milk, and maple syrup until smooth.
2. Pour the mixture into popsicle molds, leaving a little room at the top.
3. Sprinkle shredded coconut into each mold for texture, if desired.
4. Insert sticks and freeze for 4-6 hours, until solid.
5. Run warm water over the outside of the molds to release the popsicles. Serve immediately.

Dairy-Free Chocolate Tarts

Ingredients:

- 1 pre-made vegan tart shell
- 1/2 cup dairy-free chocolate chips
- 1/4 cup coconut milk
- 1 tbsp maple syrup
- 1/2 tsp vanilla extract

Instructions:

1. Preheat oven to 350°F (175°C) and bake the tart shell according to package instructions.
2. In a saucepan, heat the coconut milk and maple syrup until just simmering.
3. Pour over the chocolate chips and stir until smooth.
4. Stir in vanilla extract and pour the chocolate mixture into the baked tart shell.
5. Refrigerate for 2 hours or until the filling is set.
6. Serve chilled, optionally garnished with fresh berries or coconut flakes.

Peach Crisp with Oat Topping

Ingredients:

- 4 cups fresh peaches, peeled and sliced
- 1/4 cup maple syrup or coconut sugar
- 1 tsp vanilla extract
- 1 tbsp lemon juice
- 1 cup rolled oats
- 1/2 cup almond flour
- 1/4 cup coconut oil, melted
- 1/4 cup almond milk
- 1/4 tsp ground cinnamon
- Pinch of salt

Instructions:

1. Preheat the oven to 350°F (175°C). Grease a baking dish.
2. In a bowl, toss the sliced peaches with maple syrup, vanilla extract, and lemon juice.
3. In another bowl, combine oats, almond flour, cinnamon, and salt. Add melted coconut oil and almond milk, stirring until well combined.
4. Spread the peach mixture evenly in the baking dish and top with the oat mixture.
5. Bake for 35-40 minutes, or until the topping is golden and the peaches are bubbling.
6. Serve warm, optionally with dairy-free ice cream or whipped cream.

Almond Joy Energy Balls

Ingredients:

- 1 cup almonds, finely chopped
- 1/2 cup unsweetened shredded coconut
- 1/4 cup dark chocolate chips
- 2 tbsp maple syrup
- 1 tbsp almond butter
- 1/2 tsp vanilla extract
- Pinch of salt

Instructions:

1. In a large bowl, combine almonds, shredded coconut, dark chocolate chips, maple syrup, almond butter, vanilla extract, and salt.
2. Mix until all ingredients are evenly combined.
3. Roll the mixture into small balls, about 1-inch in diameter.
4. Place the balls on a parchment-lined tray and refrigerate for 30 minutes, or until firm.
5. Store in an airtight container in the fridge.

Vegan Lemon Coconut Bars

Ingredients:

- 1 1/2 cups shredded coconut
- 1/4 cup coconut oil, melted
- 1/4 cup maple syrup
- 2 tbsp lemon juice
- Zest of 1 lemon
- Pinch of salt

Instructions:

1. Preheat the oven to 350°F (175°C). Grease a small baking dish.
2. In a food processor, combine shredded coconut, coconut oil, maple syrup, lemon juice, lemon zest, and salt.
3. Pulse until the mixture is well combined and sticks together.
4. Press the mixture evenly into the prepared baking dish.
5. Bake for 15-20 minutes, until golden on top.
6. Let cool completely before cutting into bars.

Cashew Cream Pie

Ingredients:

- 1 1/2 cups raw cashews, soaked for 4 hours
- 1/2 cup coconut milk
- 1/4 cup maple syrup
- 1 tbsp lemon juice
- 1 tsp vanilla extract
- 1 pre-made vegan graham cracker crust

Instructions:

1. Drain the soaked cashews and place them in a blender.
2. Add coconut milk, maple syrup, lemon juice, and vanilla extract. Blend until smooth and creamy.
3. Pour the cashew cream mixture into the prepared crust.
4. Refrigerate for at least 4 hours, or until set.
5. Serve chilled, optionally topped with fresh fruit or coconut flakes.

Chocolate Coconut Energy Balls

Ingredients:

- 1 cup unsweetened shredded coconut
- 1/4 cup cocoa powder
- 1/4 cup almond butter
- 2 tbsp maple syrup
- 1/4 tsp vanilla extract
- Pinch of salt

Instructions:

1. In a large bowl, combine shredded coconut, cocoa powder, almond butter, maple syrup, vanilla extract, and salt.
2. Stir until the mixture is well combined.
3. Roll into small balls, about 1 inch in diameter.
4. Place the balls on a parchment-lined tray and refrigerate for 30 minutes.
5. Store in an airtight container in the fridge.

Apple Sorbet

Ingredients:

- 4 cups fresh apples, peeled and chopped
- 1/4 cup maple syrup or honey
- 1 tbsp lemon juice

Instructions:

1. Blend the apples, maple syrup, and lemon juice in a blender until smooth.
2. Pour the mixture into a shallow dish and freeze for 4-6 hours.
3. Every 30 minutes, scrape the mixture with a fork to break up any ice crystals.
4. Once frozen and fluffy, serve immediately or store in the freezer.

Vegan Chocolate Cupcakes

Ingredients:

- 1 1/2 cups all-purpose flour
- 1/4 cup cocoa powder
- 1 tsp baking powder
- 1/2 tsp baking soda
- 1/4 tsp salt
- 1/2 cup almond milk
- 1/4 cup vegetable oil
- 1/2 cup maple syrup
- 1 tsp vanilla extract
- 1 tbsp apple cider vinegar

Instructions:

1. Preheat the oven to 350°F (175°C) and line a muffin tin with paper liners.
2. In a large bowl, combine flour, cocoa powder, baking powder, baking soda, and salt.
3. In another bowl, mix almond milk, oil, maple syrup, vanilla extract, and apple cider vinegar.
4. Pour the wet ingredients into the dry ingredients and stir until just combined.
5. Divide the batter evenly among the muffin cups.
6. Bake for 18-20 minutes, or until a toothpick comes out clean.
7. Let cool before frosting or serving.

Dairy-Free Coffee Ice Cream

Ingredients:

- 1 can (13.5 oz) full-fat coconut milk
- 1/2 cup brewed coffee, cooled
- 1/4 cup maple syrup
- 1 tsp vanilla extract
- Pinch of salt

Instructions:

1. In a blender, combine coconut milk, brewed coffee, maple syrup, vanilla extract, and salt.
2. Blend until smooth and well combined.
3. Pour the mixture into an ice cream maker and churn according to the manufacturer's instructions.
4. Transfer to a container and freeze for 3-4 hours until firm.
5. Serve and enjoy!

Chocolate Avocado Mousse

Ingredients:

- 2 ripe avocados, peeled and pitted
- 1/4 cup cocoa powder
- 1/4 cup maple syrup
- 1 tsp vanilla extract
- Pinch of salt

Instructions:

1. Blend the avocados, cocoa powder, maple syrup, vanilla extract, and salt in a food processor until smooth and creamy.
2. Taste and adjust sweetness if needed.
3. Refrigerate for at least 1 hour before serving.
4. Serve topped with berries, coconut flakes, or a drizzle of melted chocolate.

Vegan Peanut Butter Cups

Ingredients:

- 1 cup peanut butter (creamy or crunchy)
- 1/4 cup maple syrup or agave syrup
- 1 tsp vanilla extract
- 1/4 tsp sea salt
- 1 cup dark chocolate chips (dairy-free)

Instructions:

1. Line a mini muffin tin with paper liners.
2. In a bowl, mix the peanut butter, maple syrup, vanilla extract, and sea salt until smooth.
3. Spoon a small amount of the peanut butter mixture into each muffin cup, pressing down gently to flatten.
4. Melt the dark chocolate chips in a heatproof bowl over a pot of simmering water or in the microwave.
5. Spoon a small amount of the melted chocolate over the peanut butter mixture in each cup, smoothing it out.
6. Refrigerate for at least 1 hour, or until the chocolate has hardened.
7. Store in the fridge and enjoy!

Coconut Raspberry Tart

Ingredients:

- 1 1/2 cups almond flour
- 1/4 cup shredded coconut
- 2 tbsp maple syrup
- 1/4 cup coconut oil, melted
- 1 1/2 cups fresh raspberries
- 1/4 cup coconut cream
- 2 tbsp maple syrup (for the filling)
- 1/2 tsp vanilla extract
- Pinch of sea salt

Instructions:

1. Preheat the oven to 350°F (175°C).
2. In a food processor, combine almond flour, shredded coconut, maple syrup, and melted coconut oil.
3. Pulse until the mixture resembles wet sand. Press the mixture into the bottom of a tart pan to form the crust.
4. Bake the crust for 8-10 minutes, until lightly golden. Let it cool completely.
5. In a blender, combine coconut cream, maple syrup, vanilla extract, and sea salt. Blend until smooth.
6. Pour the coconut cream mixture into the cooled tart crust.
7. Top with fresh raspberries and refrigerate for at least 2 hours before serving.

Dairy-Free Blueberry Muffins

Ingredients:

- 1 1/2 cups all-purpose flour
- 1/2 cup almond flour
- 1/4 cup coconut sugar
- 2 tsp baking powder
- 1/2 tsp baking soda
- 1/4 tsp salt
- 1/2 cup almond milk
- 1/4 cup coconut oil, melted
- 1/4 cup maple syrup
- 1 tsp vanilla extract
- 1 cup fresh blueberries

Instructions:

1. Preheat the oven to 350°F (175°C). Line a muffin tin with paper liners.
2. In a large bowl, mix together the flours, coconut sugar, baking powder, baking soda, and salt.
3. In a separate bowl, whisk together almond milk, melted coconut oil, maple syrup, and vanilla extract.
4. Add the wet ingredients to the dry ingredients and stir until just combined.
5. Gently fold in the blueberries.
6. Spoon the batter into the muffin cups, filling each about 3/4 full.
7. Bake for 18-20 minutes, or until a toothpick comes out clean.
8. Let cool for 10 minutes before removing from the tin.

Watermelon Sorbet

Ingredients:

- 4 cups fresh watermelon, chopped and seeded
- 1/4 cup lime juice
- 2 tbsp maple syrup or agave syrup
- Pinch of sea salt

Instructions:

1. In a blender, combine watermelon, lime juice, maple syrup, and salt. Blend until smooth.
2. Pour the mixture into a shallow dish and freeze for 3-4 hours.
3. Every 30 minutes, scrape the mixture with a fork to break up any ice crystals.
4. Once the sorbet is frozen and fluffy, serve immediately or store in the freezer.

Vegan Chocolate Chip Blondies

Ingredients:

- 1 cup almond flour
- 1/2 cup coconut sugar
- 1/4 tsp baking soda
- 1/4 tsp salt
- 1/4 cup almond butter
- 1/4 cup maple syrup
- 1 tsp vanilla extract
- 1/2 cup dairy-free chocolate chips

Instructions:

1. Preheat the oven to 350°F (175°C). Grease an 8x8-inch baking dish.
2. In a bowl, combine almond flour, coconut sugar, baking soda, and salt.
3. In a separate bowl, mix together almond butter, maple syrup, and vanilla extract.
4. Add the wet ingredients to the dry ingredients and stir until fully combined.
5. Fold in the chocolate chips.
6. Pour the batter into the prepared baking dish and spread it evenly.
7. Bake for 20-25 minutes, or until a toothpick comes out clean.
8. Let cool completely before cutting into squares.

Lemon Poppy Seed Cake

Ingredients:

- 1 1/2 cups all-purpose flour
- 1/2 cup almond flour
- 1/2 cup coconut sugar
- 1 tsp baking powder
- 1/2 tsp baking soda
- 1/4 tsp salt
- 1/4 cup lemon juice
- 1/4 cup almond milk
- 1/2 cup coconut oil, melted
- 1 tbsp lemon zest
- 1 tsp vanilla extract

Instructions:

1. Preheat the oven to 350°F (175°C). Grease and flour a 9-inch round cake pan.
2. In a large bowl, whisk together the flour, almond flour, coconut sugar, baking powder, baking soda, and salt.
3. In a separate bowl, combine lemon juice, almond milk, melted coconut oil, lemon zest, and vanilla extract.
4. Add the wet ingredients to the dry ingredients and stir until smooth.
5. Gently fold in the poppy seeds.
6. Pour the batter into the prepared cake pan and smooth the top.
7. Bake for 25-30 minutes or until a toothpick comes out clean.
8. Allow the cake to cool before serving.

Apple Cinnamon Donuts

Ingredients:

- 1 1/2 cups all-purpose flour
- 1/2 cup coconut flour
- 1 tsp baking soda
- 1/2 tsp cinnamon
- 1/4 tsp nutmeg
- 1/4 tsp salt
- 1/2 cup unsweetened applesauce
- 1/4 cup maple syrup
- 1/4 cup almond milk
- 1 tsp vanilla extract
- 1/2 cup diced apples (peeled)
- Coconut oil for greasing

Instructions:

1. Preheat the oven to 350°F (175°C). Grease a donut pan with coconut oil.
2. In a large bowl, whisk together the flour, coconut flour, baking soda, cinnamon, nutmeg, and salt.
3. In a separate bowl, mix together applesauce, maple syrup, almond milk, and vanilla extract.
4. Pour the wet ingredients into the dry ingredients and stir until just combined.
5. Fold in the diced apples.
6. Spoon the batter into the donut pan, filling each cavity about 3/4 full.
7. Bake for 12-15 minutes, or until a toothpick comes out clean.
8. Let the donuts cool in the pan for 5 minutes before transferring them to a wire rack.

Vegan Mocha Pudding Cake

Ingredients:

- 1 cup all-purpose flour
- 1/2 cup coconut sugar
- 1/4 cup cocoa powder
- 1 tsp baking powder
- 1/2 tsp salt
- 1/2 cup almond milk
- 1/4 cup coconut oil, melted
- 1 tbsp instant coffee granules
- 1 tsp vanilla extract
- 1/4 cup dairy-free chocolate chips

Instructions:

1. Preheat the oven to 350°F (175°C). Grease a small baking dish or ramekins.
2. In a large bowl, combine flour, coconut sugar, cocoa powder, baking powder, and salt.
3. In a separate bowl, whisk together almond milk, melted coconut oil, instant coffee, and vanilla extract.
4. Add the wet ingredients to the dry ingredients and stir until smooth.
5. Pour the batter into the prepared baking dish.
6. Sprinkle chocolate chips on top of the batter.
7. Bake for 25-30 minutes, or until the top is set and a toothpick comes out clean.
8. Let cool for a few minutes before serving.

Dairy-Free Chocolate Covered Almonds

Ingredients:

- 1 cup raw almonds
- 1/2 cup dairy-free dark chocolate chips
- 1 tbsp coconut oil
- 1/4 tsp sea salt

Instructions:

1. Line a baking sheet with parchment paper.
2. Melt the dark chocolate chips and coconut oil in a heatproof bowl over a pot of simmering water or in the microwave. Stir until smooth.
3. Dip each almond into the melted chocolate, coating it completely.
4. Place the chocolate-covered almonds on the prepared baking sheet.
5. Sprinkle a pinch of sea salt on top of each almond.
6. Refrigerate for at least 1 hour, or until the chocolate has hardened.
7. Store in an airtight container in the fridge.

www.ingramcontent.com/pod-product-compliance
Lightning Source LLC
LaVergne TN
LVHW081335060526
838201LV00055B/2663